DATE		
JAN 1992		
10 APR 1995		
14 MAY 1997		
23 FEB 2000		
22 FEB 2002		
09 SEP 2003		

MERLIN THE WIZARD

Retold by Ann Lawrence

Illustrated by Susan Hunter

Raintree Childrens Books
Milwaukee
Belitha Press Limited • London

First published in the United States of America 1986
by Raintree Publishers Inc.
310 West Wisconsin Avenue, Milwaukee, Wisconsin 53203,
in association with Belitha Press Ltd, London.

Conceived, designed and produced by Belitha Press Ltd,
31 Newington Green, London N16 9PU

Cover printed in the United States; body printed by South China
Printing, Hong Kong; bound in the United States of America.
1 2 3 4 5 6 7 8 9   89 88 87 86

11/88 B&T $15.33

Library of Congress Cataloging in Publication Data
Lawrence, Ann, 1942-
  Merlin the wizard.

  (Raintree stories)
  Based on Sir Thomas Malory's *Le morte d'Arthur.*
  Summary: A retelling of the prophecies and magical
powers of Merlin, the famous magician in the Arthurian
legend.
  1. Arthurian romances. [1. Arthur, King. 2. Merlin—
Folklore. 3. Knights and knighthood—Folklore.
4. Folklore—England] I. Hunter, Susan, ill.
II. Malory, Thomas, Sir, 15th cent. Morte d'Arthur.
Selections. III. Title.
PZ8.1.L3435Me   1986   398.2'2 [E]   86-6749
ISBN 0-8172-2628-1 (lib. bdg.)
ISBN 0-8172-2636-2 (softcover)

It was a time of violence and unrest in Britain. The Romans, who had ruled the Britons for four hundred years, had gone home to deal with trouble in Italy. In their absence, Vortigern, a British prince, made himself King. The rightful king was killed, but his two young brothers, Aurelius Ambrosius and Uther, escaped to Brittany, the country we now call France.

Vortigern invited the Saxons, a tough German clan, to Britain to help him drive out other troublesome, warring tribes. But still he lived in constant fear for his own life. He worried that the young princes, the rightful heirs to the British throne, would return. And the Saxons, led by Hengist, turned out to be a rebellious people who caused him much trouble. Finally, after a bloody battle, Vortigern was forced to give up his kingdom to the Saxons in exchange for his life. He fled to Wales for safety.

There he was advised by his magicians to build a great fortress. But when his workers began to lay the foundation, it sank into the earth each night. So Vortigern's magicians told him a sacrifice must be made. The foundation would hold firm if it was sprinkled with the blood of a boy who had never had a father.

In south Wales, in a town called Demetia, the King's messengers found a boy named Merlin. No one knew who his father was. Some said the boy was the son of a devil. But his mother was the daughter of the King of Demetia and lived in a convent in the town.

The boy and his mother were brought before Vortigern. When the King questioned Merlin's mother, she told of a mysterious stranger who had visited her in the convent. He seemed more ghostly than human. At times he talked to her without being visible at all. Some time later, they had a son.

5

When Vortigern heard this story, he didn't know whether to believe it. He asked the wisest man at his court if the story could be true. The wise man said, "There are certain spirits living between the earth and moon, which are partly like men and partly like angels. It seems they can take human shape, and it is quite possible that one could have fathered this boy."

Then the King told Merlin that he was to be made a sacrifice. At that the boy cried, "Fetch your magicians and I'll prove them liars! This isn't a matter of magic, but of engineering!"

Merlin asked the magicians, "Have you dug beneath the foundation to see what is making it sink?"

When the magicians didn't reply, the boy went on, "Lord King, order your men to dig where you are trying to build your fortress. You will find a pool, which is making the ground unstable. Drain the pool. At the bottom you will find two hollow stones, in which two dragons are sleeping." His voice sounded strange and the words seemed to come against his will.

As Vortigern and Merlin stood above the drained pool, two dragons, one red and one white, came out of the stones and began to fight. First one seemed to be winning, then the other. But it soon became clear that the white dragon would win.

"What does it mean?" the King whispered.

8

Merlin wept. "The red dragon is the people of Britain," he said. "The white one is the Saxons, who will conquer them."

Then he fell into a trance and foretold many things in strange images, which no one understood. When at last he was silent, everyone present was astonished and filled with fear, for they knew he had magical powers.

When Vortigern asked to know his own fate, Merlin replied, "You don't need me to tell you that two dangers threaten you. The Saxons are raising an army against you, and Aurelius and Uther are even now landing in Britain."

In the excitement that followed his prophesying, Merlin slipped away from Vortigern's court unnoticed. What he had predicted soon came true.

News arrived of Aurelius Ambrosius' return to Britain. The Britons welcomed him, and he was crowned King. He and Uther searched out Vortigern and burned him in his tower. Then the two brothers turned their attention to Hengist. After a long and bitter battle, they killed him and drove the Saxons to the far north.

With peace restored, Aurelius rode throughout his kingdom and ordered that towns be rebuilt. When he came to the city now called Salisbury, he was shown a place where many British leaders had been killed by the Saxons. He decided to build a monument there, but could not think of one noble enough.

He was advised to consult with Merlin, whose magical powers had astonished Vortigern. The King's messengers were sent to search for the wizard. Finally they found him wandering near a forest spring.

Merlin advised Aurelius to bring the Giants' Dance, now known as Stonehenge, from Ireland to Britain. But his idea for a monument only made the King laugh.

"Even if it could be done, why should we want to?" Aurelius cried. "Aren't there enough big stones in Britain?"

Merlin scolded the King for laughing. Then he explained that giants of old had carried the huge stones from farthest Africa and had set them up in Ireland. The stones, he said, had religious meaning and healing powers. His argument convinced the King. Aurelius sent a group of armed men, led by Uther and Merlin, to bring back the Giants' Dance.

They sailed for Ireland. But when they landed, they were met by the Irish king and his army. The Britons defeated the Irish in battle and marched on to Mount Killaraus.

There they stood in awe at the circle of huge stones. It seemed at first as if it would be impossible to move them. But Merlin used his engineering skills and magical powers. He devised a way to transport the stones to the ship, and the Britons sailed home with their precious cargo. At Salisbury, Merlin engineered the raising of the huge monument.

The King was so impressed with Merlin's powers that he kept him at court from that time on.

News came that the King of Ireland had raised an army against Britain. Aurelius was ill, so Uther and Merlin went to meet the enemy. As they were marching, there appeared in the sky a ball of fire in the shape of a dragon. From it, a ray of light stretched across the sky. When Uther asked Merlin what the sign meant, Merlin wept.

"Aurelius Ambrosius is dead," he said. "The dragon symbolizes you. You will be the ruler of all Britain. The beam of light is your son, who will be the greatest warrior ever known."

When the victorious Uther returned home, he learned that Aurelius had been poisoned, as Merlin had said. Uther was crowned King. He carried a standard with a dragon's head emblazoned on it and became known as Uther Pendragon, which meant "Dragon's head."

Soon after, the Duke of Cornwall and his wife Igraine were invited to Uther's court. Igraine was the most beautiful woman in Britain. The King fell in love with her and could think of nothing else. When the Duke and Duchess realized this, they fled Uther's court. The King was furious and ordered them to return. But they refused, and he swore revenge.

The Duke took his wife to Tintagel, his strongest castle. Then he went to a nearby fortress which the King's men soon attacked.

But Uther's love for Igraine continued to torment him. He went to Merlin for advice. The wizard thought of a plan. He agreed to change Uther's appearance so that he looked like the Duke. That way he would be admitted to Tintagel castle without question. But in return, the King must promise to give the son that he and Igraine would have to Merlin to raise. Uther agreed to these terms and went to the castle.

During that same night, the Duke of Cornwall was killed. When Igraine heard the news, she wondered who it was that had come to her since it had not been her husband. Much later, Uther admitted he had visited her that night.

Soon after the Duke's death, Uther and Igraine were married. When their son was born, Merlin came to take the child away. He was given to a knight called Sir Ector, who raised the boy as if he were his own. Merlin did this to keep the child safe because he knew the King would soon die.

Within two years, Uther became gravely ill. On his deathbed he spoke of his son Arthur. But no one had heard of him, so it seemed as if there were no rightful heir to the throne.

In the years that followed, Merlin went about his own affairs and was seldom seen. Arthur grew up and was taught the skills of knighthood by Sir Ector.

Then one year, the Archbishop of Canterbury summoned all the lords of Britain to London. Among them was fifteen-year-old Arthur. Of all those who tried, only Arthur was able to pull a mighty sword from a stone in the churchyard there. This show of strength proved him to be the rightful King of Britain, as Merlin had foreseen.

During the early years of Arthur's reign, Merlin taught the young King many things. He offered him political advice and counseled him in matters of war. On one occasion, Arthur was badly hurt while jousting with another king, Pellinore. Merlin cast a spell on Pellinore, causing him to fall asleep. Then the wizard took Arthur to a hermitage where he could rest and have his wounds tended. When it came time to leave, Arthur noticed he had lost his sword.

ut Merlin told Arthur not to worry because there was a sword nearby that he could have. Soon they came to a lake. In the middle of the lake was an arm clothed in white which held up a sword that shone in the sunlight. As Arthur watched in amazement, a young lady began to walk across the lake.

"Who is that?" Arthur asked.

"That is Nimue, the Lady of the Lake," said Merlin. "If you speak to her politely, she may give you the sword."

When the lady came near, Arthur greeted her and said he wished the sword might be his because he had none. She told him if he would get into the boat at the water's edge and row out to the sword, he could have it. And that is how Arthur got his famous sword Excalibur.

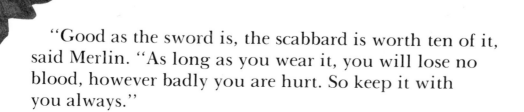

"Good as the sword is, the scabbard is worth ten of it, said Merlin. "As long as you wear it, you will lose no blood, however badly you are hurt. So keep it with you always."

Not long after this, Arthur married Guinevere. Merlin knew of the unhappiness this marriage would bring to the King, and he warned Arthur. But he also knew Arthur loved Guinevere too much to give her up for any reason.

Guinevere's father gave Arthur the Round Table as a wedding present. Merlin helped him choose the best, most noble knights to sit at it. Among them was Pellinore, now a friend of the King. Pellinore came to court with the beautiful Nimue, whom he had rescued from great danger.

Nimue was an enchantress. She was already wise and skilled in many of the magic arts. But she wished to learn more from Merlin. At first, he taught her simple things, how to create rivers and magic gardens in the forest. But when he saw she truly wanted to learn his great powers, he fell in love with her. He began to teach her all that he knew, and she loved him in return. They wandered the world together, spending ever less time at court. Merlin warned King Arthur that a time would come when he would not return.

In her jealous love for him, Nimue asked Merlin to teach her how to tie a man so that only she could free him. Merlin taught her the spell, although he knew how she meant to use it.

One day they strayed far into the forest of Broceliande. They sat beneath a hawthorn tree to rest. When Merlin fell asleep, Nimue wrapped her veil around the tree and walked around it nine times, whispering the words Merlin had taught her.

When Merlin awoke he seemed to be lying on a bed in a high tower. He knew at once that Nimue had cast a spell on him. She stayed near him, and after a time, was sorry for what she had done and would have freed him. But the spell was too strong; she could not break it.

For a long time, Arthur's court heard no news of Merlin. Then one day, Sir Gawain, one of the King's knights, was riding through the forest. He heard a voice like wind rustling the leaves, calling his name. The frightened knight recognized Merlin's voice and begged the wizard to show himself. Merlin replied that no one would ever see or hear him again, and that he was a prisoner in this place. When Gawain asked how this could have happened to the wisest of men, Merlin explained, "I am also the greatest fool. I taught my love to bind me to her, and now I can never be free."

As for Arthur, everything that Merlin foretold came true. He was much loved by his people and ruled for some years in peace. His knights righted wrongs and did chivalrous deeds. But after a time, the King's queen and his best knight betrayed him. His own son led the Saxons against him, and Arthur was killed by him in battle.

Merlin had made one final prophecy—that both he and Arthur would wake and return to Britain in its hour of greatest need. But until then, Merlin sleeps, watched by Nimue, in his invisible tower.